UMOREN KOKO

John 1:17 – KJV
For the law was given by Moses, but grace and
truth came by Jesus Christ.

FINDING
GRACE

FINDING
GRACE

UMOREN KOKO

ISBN   978-978-59058-4-7

Published in Nigeria by
WIND CHILD

Copyright © Umoren Koko 2023

All scriptures are taken from the King James Version of the Bible. This version was preferred because it is an earlier version than most of the other versions of the Bible in circulation.

Many other versions are basically interpretations and translations of the KJV. Therefore, to avoid this work being influenced by a third party's interpretation or translation, the KJV became the preferred Bible.

CONTENTS

DEDICATION

This book is dedicated to you the reader.

INTRODUCTION

Where I come from (Lagos Nigeria), one of the most used words whether in real-life conversations or on social media platforms is the word 'grace'. Used by pastors, churchgoers, Imams, Muslims, atheists, fraudsters, traditionalists, and almost everyone.

The widespread use of the word should be a surprise to anyone because this word subconsciously is widely perceived to have its origin from the Christian faith. So, it is understandable when you see a devoted Christian blot out the word for whatever purpose.

According to the book of John, the word Grace is something that a Christian now has access to because of Jesus.

John 1:17 — KJV

17. For the law was given by Moses, but grace and truth came by Jesus Christ.

Postulating that Moses might have brought laws for the children of Israel but Jesus brought grace. This has formed the foundation for a widespread Christian belief that grace is now something that can be accessed because of the existence of Jesus. Meaning that it was not accessible before Jesus.

If the present common knowledge about the word grace is borrowed from Christianity, why then is it freely being used by almost everyone?

In today's world, you come across people who are known to be largely fraudsters who swindle people for money and engage in any illegal activities for money, referencing the word Grace as the reason why they have been able to amass their ill-gotten wealth. It isn't just fraudsters, but almost everyone.

Nowadays, grace has also been seen as a license or covering for sin. Many people go about doing evil and when you challenge their actions, they tell you we are covered by grace or we are in the dispensation of grace. This should leave any honest mind wandering how something claimed to be ushered in by Jesus, could be used as a cove or justification for evil. How can something made available by Jesus (the epitome of righteousness in Christianity) be cited as an ally in fraud and a cover for unrighteousness?

I have tried to accept this widespread perception towards grace but it doesn't hold up. Simply because God dislikes sin and cannot create a provision for sin to be overlooked.

Thus, if this is not grace, what then is grace?

12

GRACE

Modern Christianity

A lot of Christians today would define grace as an 'unmerited favour' when asked. This means that grace is God choosing to favour an individual even though such an individual has not merited being favoured.

Perhaps this is the reason why even criminals feel entitled to grace. Because they know that God does not approve of their actions, so when they get away with their actions, they say it was because of grace that they have been favoured even when they did not merit it.

It is very difficult to trace when or who translated grace to mean unmerited favour but for some reason, we have come to terms with this definition. This definition tends to paint God as someone with some level of bias towards some individuals and bias against some individuals.

I find this definition disturbing because it creates room for some people to feel that God doesn't love or favour them anytime things go bad for them. This is a very risky mindset to get trapped in.

The question is 'is God biased?' and the answer is no.

Matthew 5:45 - KJV

45. That ye may be the children of your Father which is in heaven: for he maketh his sun to rise on the evil and on the good, and sendeth rain on the just and on the unjust.

It is clear from this passage that God is not biased or grants anyone favours that they do not merit.

In these verses, Jesus makes it clear that God doesn't deal partially with people and he acts justly. Thus, the idea that God developed a preference for those who claim to be followers of Jesus is simply false. Thus, the idea that the grace that Jesus brought is unmerited favour, doesn't hold up under scrutiny.

Another religious view on grace is that Jesus brought in a period of grace where those who profess that Jesus is their Lord and personal saviour are automatically exempted from the consequences of sin. Therefore, they can continue living as they please. But this is a very dangerous misinterpretation of the grace that Jesus brought.

If you observe societies that buy into this kind of teaching, you would notice the prevalence of mental illness, drug abuse, sex abuse, suicide, divorce, lack of peace in homes amongst other symptoms that indicate that their souls are dying. This is the story of modern-day Christian society. Perhaps this misinterpretation of grace is at the centre of the decay in Christian societies. Rather than find a way to righteousness, many now believe that once they can say a prayer of repentance, they are covered by grace and can therefore continue living in sin. The other problem with this interpretation of grace is that it leads people to the conclusion that righteousness is impossible but is this what God thinks?

Leviticus 11:44

44. For I am the LORD your God: ye shall therefore sanctify yourselves, and ye shall be holy; for I am holy: neither shall ye defile yourselves with any manner of creeping thing that creepeth upon the earth.

1 Peter 1:16 - KJV

16. Because it is written, Be ye holy; for I am holy.

Matthew 5:48 - KJV

48. Be ye therefore perfect, even as your Father which is in heaven is perfect.

Therefore, any doctrine that creates the notion that God has created a way to cover up for sin because it is impossible to be righteous/holy/perfect is contradicting the bible and should not claim to be speaking as a disciple of Jesus.

So, if these interpretations of grace are wrong, then what is the correct meaning of grace? The answer is in the dictionary.

There is a constant reoccurrence in religion where religious leaders change the meanings of words. A word that existed before Christianity and was used by Jesus and his disciples suddenly has a different meaning in modern Christianity.

The original meaning of the word grace is to do something with ease. For example, we can say that a soccer player plays with so much grace. This means that the player plays with so much ease or effortlessness or finesse. If you say someone speaks with grace, you are therefore saying they speak with elegance, effortlessness, finesse, and eloquence. Grace is the ability to do something that otherwise would be difficult, but to do it with ease.

I first realized this definition of Grace when I was watching a lawn tennis match on TV which involved the great swede, Rodger Federer. He was playing with difficult techniques and he made them look so easy to accomplish. Then I heard the commentator say he was playing with so much grace.

Born into a typical Christian background, I was shocked to hear the word grace used in a tennis match so I immediately ran and picked up a dictionary to confirm if the commentator had applied the word correctly. It was there It dawned on me that the word grace was not a Christian word but a normal word that existed on its own. This word was not invented by Christians although it now appears as though Christianity coined the word grace. In fact, at the time the word was being written in either Hebrew or Greek in the bible, Christianity was not an existing religion. Therefore, it is wrong to now use the modern Christian definition to interpret ancient texts. Perhaps we will be best served to stick to the circular translation of the word Grace.

If we take this circular meaning of grace into the scripture, grace therefore means to live a righteous life with ease or effortlessness, or finesse.

Therefore, John was saying that while Moses brought laws Jesus made it easier to fulfil these laws

John 1:17 - KJV

17.   For the law was given by Moses, but grace and truth came by Jesus Christ.

Thus because of Jesus, we should now be able to live the life of God with ease. This makes more sense when compared to the modern Christian application of the word Grace. Especially when you consider 2 Peter 1:1-4

2 Peter 1:1 – 4 – KJV

1. Simon Peter, a servant and an apostle of Jesus Christ, to them that have obtained like precious faith with us through the righteousness of God and our Saviour Jesus Christ:

2. Grace and peace be multiplied unto you through the knowledge of God, and of Jesus our Lord,

3. According as his divine power hath given unto us all things that pertain unto life and godliness, through the knowledge of him that hath called us to glory and virtue:

4. Whereby are given unto us exceeding great and precious promises: that by these ye might be partakers of the divine nature, having escaped the corruption that is in the world through lust.

Here peter seems to agree that grace gives us the ability to partake in the divine nature of God. Meaning that there is a correlation between Grace and living righteously.

Grace is therefore more of power/ability than unmerited favour. Therefore, the grace of God is the power of God in someone's life that will help them achieve things easier/effortlessly than normal.

There are still parts of the bible (especially the early parts of the bible) where the use of the word grace is to reflect favour from God to man. But in these passages, the Hebrew word used is חֵן (*ḥen*) as seen in Genesis 6:8. This word can be translated to mean charm, grace, likeability, or appeal.

You must realize that to build likeability, appeal or to be able to charm someone is not unmerited, you must have or are doing something. For example, in Genesis 6:8 it is said that Noah found grace in the sight of God. But it wasn't unmerited, Noah was a righteous and upright man who obeyed God.

Genesis 6:8 - KJV

8.   But Noah found grace in the eyes of the LORD.

This verse is simply saying that God was impressed with Noah. The reason is in the next verse.

Genesis 6:9 – KJV

9.   These are the generations of Noah: Noah was a just man and perfect in his generations, and Noah walked with God.

So even if one was to argue that grace is favour because of the use in this verse, you can't argue that it was unmerited.

Genesis 19:18-19 – KJV

18.   And Lot said unto them, Oh, not so, my Lord:

19.   Behold now, thy servant hath found grace in thy sight, and thou hast magnified thy mercy, which thou hast shewed unto me in saving my life; and I cannot escape to the mountain, lest some evil take me, and I die:

This story is about a man named Lot who had just been saved from the destruction of Sodom and Gomorrah. And he was thanking God for finding Grace in him.

The story trumps the idea that grace is unmerited favour because Lot was only spared because he was found to be righteous and kind. He had made effort to save the angels of God who were in Sodom and Gomorrah from the wicked men of the city. So, the grace was merited.

But just like the case of Noah, grace is used as evidence of righteousness.

Genesis 32:3-5 - KJV

3.   And Jacob sent messengers before him to Esau his brother unto the land of Seir, the country of Edom.

4.   And he commanded them, saying, Thus shall ye speak unto my lord Esau; Thy servant Jacob saith thus, I have sojourned with Laban, and stayed there until now:

5.   And I have oxen, and asses, flocks, and menservants, and womenservants: and I have sent to tell my lord, that I may find grace in thy sight.

In the above verses, Jacob was simply trying to rebuild the relationship he once had with his older brother Esau and he sent servants with promises of gifts to his brother asking that his brother finds grace in him.

The first thing to note is that grace isn't something that only God can give although the grace of God would surpass any other grace. But if you use the translate the Hebrew word used in this verse, Jacob was only asking that his brother finds him likeable and appealing as he used to. And Jacob sort to earn this likability by first referring to himself as a servant of Esau, then informing Esau of the many flocks and servants that he has that could be of use to Esau.

Jacob was seeking to merit the grace that he sorts from his brother Esau.

This goes to show that there is nothing unmerited about the word grace. It is earned either from man or God. You have to possess/offer something to find grace. In the case of God's grace, the price has to be righteousness.

This means for God to find grace in you, you have to be righteous.

But let's not forget the modern circular application of the word grace as the ability to do something with ease.

This application of the word grace can even be found in some later uses of the word grace in the old testament.

Psalms 45:1-2 - KJV

1. My heart is inditing a good matter: I speak of the things which I have made touching the king: my tongue is the pen of a ready writer.

2. Thou art fairer than the children of men: grace is poured into thy lips: therefore, God hath blessed thee forever.

These verses seem to be speaking highly of someone who has the ability to charm with his words. Thus, the writer describes the person as having grace on his lips. This person has the ability to get things done with ease when he talks.

Psalms 84:11 - KJV

11.   For the LORD God is a sun and shield: the LORD will give grace and glory: no good thing will he withhold from them that walk uprightly.

This verse paints grace as a gift/ability/power given by God. But the catch here is that it is for those who walk uprightly (thus it is merited).

Proverb 1:7-8 - KJV

7.   The fear of the LORD is the beginning of knowledge: but fools despise wisdom and instruction.

8.   My son, hear the instruction of thy father, and forsake not the law of thy mother:

9.   For they shall be an ornament of grace unto thy head, and chains about thy neck.

This verse depicts a piece of advice given to a younger individual, saying that the instructions of his father and the laws of his mother would be like an ornament of grace, meaning that they would be a source of power to stay righteous .and they would be a 'chain about his neck' meaning that the instructions of his father and the laws of his mother would serve as a restraint that would keep him from doing evil and offending God.

This paints a positive correlation between grace and righteousness.

Proverb 3:21-23 - KJV

21.   My son, let not them depart from thine eyes: keep sound wisdom and discretion:

22.   So shall they be life unto thy soul, and grace to thy neck.

23.   Then shalt thou walk in thy way safely, and thy foot shall not stumble.

Here again, grace is depicted as the ability or power to stand steadfast.

Proverb 3:33-34 - KJV

33.   The curse of the LORD is in the house of the wicked: but he blesseth the habitation of the just.

34. Surely he scorneth the scorners: but he giveth grace unto the lowly.

Here, grace is still painted as an ability/gift given to the lowly(humble) and the Just.

These verses are in line with the modern circular interpretation of Grace as the ability to do something with ease/effortlessness/finesse.

To apply this interpretation into our spiritual life will mean the ability to live the life of God (to please God) with ease.

don't forget that by Hebrew definition, grace means to be found pleasing.

The concept of grace begins to add up. We can now boldly interpret John's statement about grace.

John 1:17 - KJV

17. For the law was given by Moses, but grace and truth came by Jesus Christ.

This means that although Moses gave us laws on how to please God, Jesus has made it much easier through his message (the truth).

Grace therefore can be defined as the ability/power to please God (live righteously) with ease.

This is what grace means; to be free from the bondage of sin. If you are not experiencing victory over sin, then you can't claim to be operating in grace.

28

29

GRACE AND RIGHTEOUSNESS

No matter how you chose to look at God's grace at this point, be it as an evidence/reward for righteousness or as a requirement for righteousness, the takeaway is that it goes hand in hand with righteousness.

Thus, the surest way to find Gods' grace is to find righteousness. We concluded earlier that grace is the ability to please God with ease. And the surest way to please God is to be righteous (as in the case of Noah).

Genesis 6:8-9 - KJV

8.   But Noah found grace in the eyes of the LORD.

9. These are the generations of Noah: Noah was a just man and perfect in his generations, and Noah walked with God.

Since the surest way to the grace of God is righteousness, then we must find the easiest way to righteousness if we are to find grace.

David in the bible was one man who seemed to know the secret to righteousness.

Psalms 111:10 - KJV

*10. The fear of the LORD is the beginning of wisdom: a good **understanding** have all they that do his commandments: his praise endureth for ever.*

Psalms 119:34 - KJV

*34. Give me **understanding,** and I shall keep thy law; yea, I shall observe it with my whole heart.*

David seems to believe that the secret ingredient to keeping the commandments of God and pleasing God is understanding.

When it comes to keeping the commandments of God, many people struggle to do so simply because they have not understood the commandments and why they exist., many people have not understood that the commandments of God are for their own good, not God's.

A good example is someone who lies and does not realize that it is his own reputation and credibility at stake, not God's.

Another example is fornication. People who disobey this do not fully grasp the consequences of their actions both to their soul and their body. God will never be at risk of any sexually transmitted disease. It is the fornicator at risk. God is never at risk of a broken marriage or relationship or broken heart. It is always the perpetrator of fornication or adultery.

There are other things to understand that will help one stay righteous easily, but the basic understanding of this is that being righteous is not for God's benefit but Man's.

Many people think that the commandments are in place for God's benefit because of the way they have been taught. They do not understand that the only reason your unrighteousness displeases God, is because he loves you and can't stand watching the consequences you have to face because of your unrighteousness.

Part of being righteous (accessing/living by grace) is being able to overcome temptations. So, if we say having understanding is the way to righteousness/grace, then understanding must also be a way to overcome temptations.

Let us examine the very first temptation in the bible (the temptation of Eve) and see if an understanding could have helped.

Genesis 3:1-7 - KJV

1.   Now the serpent was more subtle than any beast of the field which the LORD God had made. And he said unto the woman, Yea, hath God said, Ye shall not eat of every tree of the garden?
2.   And the woman said unto the serpent, We may eat of the fruit of the trees of the garden:
3.   But of the fruit of the tree which is in the midst of the garden, God hath said, Ye shall not eat of it, neither shall ye touch it, lest ye die.
4.   And the serpent said unto the woman, Ye shall not surely die:
5.   For God doth know that in the day ye eat thereof, then your eyes shall be opened, and ye shall be as gods, knowing good and evil.
6.   And when the woman saw that the tree was good for food, and that it was pleasant to the eyes, and a tree to be desired to make one wise, she took of the fruit thereof, and did eat, and gave also unto her husband with her; and he did eat.
7.   And the eyes of them both were opened, and they knew that they were naked; and they sewed fig leaves together, and made themselves aprons.

In this temptation, all the serpent did was trick the woman that if she eats from the tree of knowledge of good and evil, she will be like gods (verse 5). But this was a trick because there was no need for Eve to want to be like gods. After all, in chapter one of Genesis, it is said that she was already created in the image of the almighty God.

But the serpent was able to paint becoming a god (take note of the small letter g) as a step forward for Eve.

Genesis 1:27 - KJV

*27.   So God **created** man in his own image, in the image of God created he him; male and female created he them.*

The only reason why Eve fell for this is that she was ignorant to the fact that she was already in the image of the almighty God. At the time God decided to create man in His image, man was not in existence thus the only beings that knew that man was created in the image of God are whoever God was speaking to in Genesis 1:26.

Genesis 1:26 - KJV

26.   And God said, Let us make man in our image, after our likeness: and let them have dominion over the fish of the sea, and over the fowl of the air, and over the cattle, and over all the earth, and over every creeping thing that creepeth upon the earth.

Let's assume that Eve had already been told that she was created in the image of God, she could still have fallen for the temptation because there is a difference between knowing and understanding. So perhaps Eve did not understand how she was created in the image of God.

Many of us still lack this understanding until this day. Whenever we hear that we are created in the image of God, we automatically think that God looks physically the way we do. But that would be wrong considering that there are many imperfections in our physical body. God can't be said to have such imperfections.

So how then are we created in the image of God?

To understand this, we have to know what the image of God is.

John 4:24 - KJV

*24.   God is a **Spirit:** and they that worship him must worship him in spirit and in truth.*

God is a spirit, this is why no one has seen God physically therefore if man was created in the image of God, then man had to have been a spirit. Only that man was given a body in Genesis 2:7.

Genesis 2:6-7 - KJV

6.   But there went up a **mist** from the earth, and **watered** the whole face of the **ground.**
7.   And the LORD God formed man of the dust of the ground, and breathed into his nostrils the breath of life; and man became a living soul.

So, the serpent was only able to get Eve because Eve did not understand how she was created in the image of God. That it was a spiritual resemblance to God not physical. If she had thought that her resemblance to God was physical then that explains why it was easy to convince her that that wasn't enough because when it comes to our physical body, there are too many flaws and limitations to be able to prove that we are in the image of God.

This is why even to this day many Christians struggle to have complete confidence (faith) that they are in the image of God because they do not understand that it's not a physical image but spiritual. We do not understand that Man is a spiritual being like God only that man is housed in a physical container called the flesh. Many people do not understand that we are not our flesh.

Eve's faith failed because she lacked understanding. This shows that there is no faith without understanding.

Another example of temptation is the one joseph faced in the house of Potiphar. Potiphar's wife tried to seduce Joseph into sexual immorality but Joseph ran away even leaving his garment behind.

Genesis 39:7 - 12 - KJV

7.   And it came to pass after these things, that his master's wife cast her eyes upon Joseph; and she said, Lie with me.

8.   But he refused, and said unto his master's wife, Behold, my master wotteth not what is with me in the house, and he hath committed all that he hath to my hand;

9.   There is none greater in this house than I; neither hath he kept back any thing from me but thee, because thou art his wife: how then can I do this great wickedness, and sin against God?

10.   And it came to pass, as she spake to Joseph day by day, that he hearkened not unto her, to lie by her, or to be with her.

11.   And it came to pass about this time, that Joseph went into the house to do his business; and there was none of the men of the house there within.

12.   And she caught him by his garment, saying, Lie with me: and he left his garment in her hand, and fled, and got him out.

What saved Joseph in this temptation was that he understood that when it comes to sexual urges, the surest way to overcome is to flee(run). Don't even think about trusting your flesh in such situations, run while you still have the will to.

1 Corinthians 6:18 - KJV

18.   Flee fornication. Every sin that a man doeth is without the body; but he that committeth fornication sinneth against his own body.

2 Timothy 2:22 - KJV

22.   Flee also youthful lusts: but follow righteousness, faith, charity, peace, with them that call on the Lord out of a pure heart.

Unfortunately, many people do not understand this rule. They constantly stick around sexual temptations, trusting that they can handle them until they fall and start regretting their decisions.

Jesus was another person who used understanding(faith) to overcome temptation. His understanding of the scriptures he had read, and his understanding of what is important in life was what he used to overcome his temptations.

Matthew 4:1-10 - KJV

1.   Then was Jesus led up of the Spirit into the wilderness to be tempted of the devil.

2.   And when he had fasted forty days and forty nights, he was afterward an hungred.

3.   And when the tempter came to him, he said, If thou be the Son of God, command that these stones be made bread.

4.   But he answered and said, It is written, Man shall not live by bread alone, but by every word that proceedeth out of the mouth of God.

5.   Then the devil taketh him up into the holy city, and setteth him on a pinnacle of the temple,

6.   And saith unto him, If thou be the Son of God, cast thyself down: for it is written, He shall give his angels charge concerning thee: and in their hands they shall bear thee up, lest at any time thou dash thy foot against a stone.

7.   Jesus said unto him, It is written again, Thou shalt not tempt the Lord thy God.

8.   Again, the devil taketh him up into an exceeding high mountain, and sheweth him all the kingdoms of the world, and the glory of them;

9.   And saith unto him, All these things will I give thee, if thou wilt fall down and worship me.

10.   Then saith Jesus unto him, Get thee hence, Satan: for it is written, Thou shalt worship the Lord thy God, and him only shalt thou serve.

Most temptations occur like arguments or debates either in your head or with someone else. And if you lack knowledge and understanding, it is very difficult to win these debates. This means that without understanding, it is impossible to stay righteous, thus difficult to access the grace of God or to find grace in the sight of God.

If we say that Grace is the ability to please God with ease, then we are saying that without understanding, it is difficult to please God. This is true because it is difficult to please anyone you do not understand.

GRACE AND FAITH

We have defined grace as the ability to please God with ease, and we have also established the relationship between grace and righteousness which is also what pleases God. But there is also another component required to please God and this component is called faith.

Hebrew 11:6 - KJV

6.   But without faith it is impossible to please him: for he that cometh to God must believe that he is, and that he is a rewarder of them that diligently seek him.

Here we see that we need faith if we are to please God. This means that faith is a requirement for grace.

To prove this, we need to understand the concept of faith.

Circular meaning of faith

According to the dictionary, faith is defined as complete confidence in something.

Here I would like you to take note of the word "**complete**" and the word "**confidence**".

Please hold unto these two words in your mind.

Biblical meaning of faith

According to the bible, faith is defined as:

Hebrews 11:1 – KJV

1. Now faith is the substance of things hoped for, the evidence of things not seen.

Here I would like you to take note of the words "**substance**" and "**evidence**"

You also have to take note of the definition of faith in the book of Hebrew, it is telling us that faith is not hope, but the substance of the things we hope for. There is therefore a difference between faith and hope.

This definition also puts distance between faith and things that we have not seen but describes faith as the evidence of the things we have not seen.

Most times what we call faith is just us holding unto hopes and things that are unseen without any substance to our hopes or evidence to back up the unseen things we hold unto. According to Hebrew 11:1 if there is no substance or evidence, then it is not faith.

Substance:

Is the physical matter of which a person or thing consists and which has a tangible and solid presence.

This means that faith is not having hope in something but having physical and tangible proof/presence to represent your hope. This means hope becomes faith when you can use physical and

tangible matter to prove it (to provide evidence).

Evidence:

Is the available body of facts or information, indicating whether a belief or proposition is true or valid.

This means that faith is not about holding onto things that are unseen but faith is to be able to provide facts or information to show that the unseen that you hold unto is true or valid.

Therefore, faith is not about having hopes or holding onto something unseen, but faith is about being able to back up your hopes and unseen things with substance and evidence. But to provide substance or evidence to anything, you must possess an understanding of that thing.

Therefore, if there is no faith without substance and evidence, there is no faith without understanding. This means that if you can't have faith without being able to provide substance and evidence, you can't have faith in something you do not understand.

To prove that Jesus had faith, he was always able to provide substance and evidence to his teachings using real-life things as parables. He was always able to explain how his teachings affect real life. This showed that he truly understood the things he was talking about. In other words, Jesus had faith (complete confidence) in what he was talking about.

The word evidence is taken from the word evident which means obvious to the eyes. Thus, you really can't have faith in something you haven't understood to a point where you can make it obvious to the eyes.

Many people have hope that the things they have heard are right but until they can provide evidence or substance to their belief systems, all they have is hope, not faith.

Faith can't exist without these two words "Substance" and "evidence". "Substance" and "evidence" can't exist without "understanding".

Faith therefore can't exist without "understanding".

If we marry the conventional definition of faith and the definition in Hebrew, this means that to have complete confidence in a person or something, you must have an understanding of that person or something. You can't have complete confidence in who/what you do not understand. It is simply impossible.

You can hope that a thing or a person will deliver for you, but you can't have complete confidence when you do not understand that thing or that person.

You can't go into an examination with complete confidence except you have an understanding of the subject matter.

If we take another look at the biblical definition of faith.

Hebrews 11:1 – KJV

1. Now faith is the substance of things hoped for, the evidence of things not seen.

You can't give substance to things you hope for except you have understood those things.

You can't provide evidence to things unseen except you have understood them.

The summary here is that faith is standing on a foundation called understanding.

Faith = Understanding.

Remember that we have been able to establish the relationship between understanding, righteousness, and grace. Thus, if there is a direct positive relationship between understanding and faith, then there is also such a relationship between faith, grace, and righteousness. It is therefore right to say that faith, understanding, and righteousness are prerequisites for grace (the ability to please God with ease).

One way to prove this is to examine the sources of faith, righteousness, and understanding.

Romans 10:17 – KJV

17. So then faith cometh by hearing, and hearing by the word of God.

This passage shows that faith is gotten by hearing the true word of God.

Psalms 111:10 - KJV

10. The fear of the LORD is the beginning of wisdom: a good **understanding** *have all they that do his commandments: his praise endureth for ever.*

Psalms 119:34 - KJV

34. Give me **understanding,** *and I shall keep thy law; yea, I shall observe it with my whole heart.*

Understanding is the requirement for keeping the commandments of God (righteousness)

Psalms 119:130 - KJV

130. The entrance of thy words giveth light; it giveth understanding unto the simple.

The word of God also brings understanding. Therefore, the word of God is the source of understanding, righteousness, and faith. Thus, the word of God is the foundation for the grace of God. This is supported by one of our earlier vases by John.

John 1:17 – KJV

17.   For the law was given by Moses, but grace and truth came by Jesus Christ.

In this verse, the truth represents the word of God.

John 17:17 – KJV

17.   Sanctify them through thy truth: **thy word is truth.**

But the important thing to take away from John 1:17 is that John highlights that the truth came with grace. He was therefore saying that because of the truth taught by Jesus, we now have grace (find it easier to please God). This is because this truth also builds our faith (understanding). And we know from the book of Hebrew that it is impossible to please God (have God's grace) without faith (understanding).

This chapter concludes that faith (understanding) is a prerequisite for righteousness and God's grace.

50

51

BUILDING GRACE

We have already established that faith is built on understanding and is also a prerequisite for righteousness and God's grace as a result. We also have seen that understanding, as well as faith, come through the word of God. Thus, the way to achieve/get God's grace starts with understanding the word of God (the truth).

Romans 10:17 - KJV

17. So then faith cometh by hearing, and hearing by the word of God.

But the challenge with many people is that they have failed to realize that the word of God doesn't only come from pastors or via religion.

Anything true can be said to be the word of God. Because the word of God is described as the truth.

John 17:17 - KJV

17.   Sanctify them through thy truth: **thy word is truth.**

Anything that is the truth will lead to understanding.

Psalms 119:130 - KJV

130.   The entrance of thy words giveth light; it giveth understanding unto the simple.

The truth can come from anywhere. It can be your doctor, your friend, anywhere. But the litmus test for the truth is that it will give more understanding of the situation.

A doctor who gives you information about your body that is true is also giving you the word of God. A media house that gives you true information is also giving you the word of God. But with so much information that you can come across, one sure way to identify the truth is that it increases understanding (faith).

I am saying that the way to increase faith is to prioritize knowledge but not all knowledge only those that will increase your understanding. This means that you must in the first place be seeking to understand.

You must be actively seeking to know more and understand more at every time.

The truth is understanding comes from God but without an arsenal of knowledge, there is little for God to work within your life. It is the knowledge that you have that God will use to give you understanding by shedding his light on that knowledge.

If you do not have information/knowledge on the human body, God can't help you understand the human body.

If you do not have information about computers, you can't understand computers. If you are not informed about politics and economics, you can't get to understand politics and the economy. So, understanding starts with knowledge.

It is what you know that God will use to teach you deeper things. If you do not speak English God can't use English to teach you. He will use whatever language you know. God couldn't have used aeroplanes to talk to Moses because Moses did not know what an aeroplane is. So, your understanding/faith is limited by the depth of your knowledge. Without reading and knowing the text in the bible, you would never be able to understand it. So first you would need to know what is written in the bible.

Although there are those who know almost all the text in the bible but do not understand it. This is because they are not open to understanding it.

This leads us to a key ingredient of building faith/understanding which is humility. Without being humble it is difficult to admit within oneself that there could be more to understand in an issue. Many people read the bible and conclude that whatever they conclude has to be the interpretation or whatever interpretation they got from their religious leader is the right interpretation. It takes humility to stay open to anything that could contradict your view provided it increases your level of understanding. But many minds are closed thus they have the knowledge, but lack understanding.

This is why David said that understanding is given only to the simple (humble).

Psalms 119:130 - KJV

130.   The entrance of thy words giveth light; it giveth understanding unto the simple.

Thus, you can't build your faith/understanding without being humble.

The conclusion here is that to be a man/woman of faith you must be hungry for knowledge not only from the bible and you must have a humble spirit. Having knowledge outside of your religion is very vital because most times, God will use your general knowledge to help you understand your religious knowledge. Just the way Jesus used to use his knowledge on farming, politics, and other topics as parables when explaining spiritual things.

Having knowledge is the fundamental thing in life, it then gives you room to have understanding and thus increases your faith which will help you be more righteous and obtain God's grace.

Hosea 4:6 - KJV

6. My people are destroyed for lack of knowledge: because thou hast rejected knowledge, I will also reject thee, that thou shalt be no priest to me: seeing thou hast forgotten the law of thy God, I will also forget thy children.

Unfortunately, many have been fooled to believe that ignorance is bliss. Thus, they lack knowledge, so they lack the necessary foundation to get understanding, and thus have very weak faiths. This means the inability to stay righteous and experience grace.

GRACE AND CHALLENGES

One of the general feelings towards grace is that it is meant to make one's life easier especially when dealing with life's challenges. This is why even criminals claim that they have been aided by grace when they get away with their crimes. They claim to have received an unmerited favour from God.

But we have already established that there is nothing unmerited about grace. And we have also seen that God is a just God that doesn't deal partially with mankind.

Matthew 5:45 - KJV

45. That ye may be the children of your Father which is in heaven: for he maketh his sun to rise on the evil and on the good, and sendeth rain on the just and on the unjust.

But does this mean that grace doesn't make one's life easier? The answer is that it does make it easier to tackle life's challenges.

If so, then how does this work?

The answer is in the process of achieving/attaining grace; to attain grace, we have identified faith as a key component and faith is a requirement for removing mountains (overcoming challenges).

Matthew 17:20 - KJV

20.   And Jesus said unto them, Because of your unbelief: for verily I say unto you, If ye have faith as a grain of mustard seed, ye shall say unto this mountain, Remove hence to yonder place; and it shall remove; and nothing shall be impossible unto you.

This is also confirmed in another verse in the bible that agrees that faith is what is required to move mountains.

1 Corinthians 13:2 - KJV

2.   And though I have the gift of prophecy, and understand all mysteries, and all knowledge; and though I have all faith, so that I could remove mountains, and have not charity, I am nothing.

Faith gives the power to remove mountains and by mountains, we mean life's challenges.

So how then does this work? The answer is in the key element of faith 'understanding'.

Mountains are used in these verses to represent problems and challenges therefore what these verses are saying is that you will require faith to solve problems and tackle challenges. If faith is the same as understanding, these verses are saying that you will require understanding to solve problems and tackle challenges. This we can all agree with. To solve any problem, be it in your job, or family, or anywhere, you must have an understanding of the matter at hand.

Many people pray for favour or promotion in their place of work. And because they have sown some sort of seed in church or because they have hope they think they have faith. Meanwhile, their colleagues at work demonstrate a better understanding of the Job, a better understanding of the work environment, a better understanding of the people they report to, or a better understanding of the customers. By our conclusion on faith, it is the colleagues that have more faith. Thus, the colleagues are more qualified for the said promotion.

Some people may be facing mountains in their marriage and thus they turn to prayers and all sorts of religious actions but they never seek to understand marriage from God's point of view, they never seek to understand their spouse, they never seek to understand the root cause of the problem at hand. They are therefore working without faith but just hope.

Some people walk boldly into business ventures because they have consulted some religious leaders who have prayed for them, or they have sown some religious seeds, or they are banking on their religiousness. But they don't seek to have an understanding of the business, its environment, the economic climate, its potential clients, etc.

What they are working with is hope, not faith. It will be difficult for them to move mountains.

It was those with the understanding that moved mountains in transportation by inventing trains, ships, and aeroplanes. It was understanding that moved mountains and brought about electricity and many inventions. To move an actual mountain would only be made possible by understanding (faith).

Only a person with understanding can predict events, especially economic events, and plan towards them. And when good things happen easily for such a person, he or she can boldly say he took actions by faith.

Some people are claiming to have faith in the area of marriage but lack understanding of God's view on marriage and how to spot the right person for them. They don't even understand their self so can't even tell who is good for them. So, if God puts the right person in front of them, they might not know it. Yet they would say they have faith. A lot of the mistakes made in life are just down to a lack of understanding (faith).

Some people are believing God for wealth but are not seeking to understand God's principles for wealth. They don't read any books on wealth nor even study wealthy characters in their bible or real life. They have little understanding of wealth yet they claim to have faith that they will be wealthy. Faith can't work without understanding.

It is hard for anyone searching for wealth without understanding to trust his/her process thus when any trial or test arises, they will shake and try to help themselves out by either committing a crime or looking for a shortcut to wealth. It will be hard for such a person to uphold their righteousness in the face of temptation.

Even the idea of praying with faith is better understood when you swap faith for understanding. This becomes praying with understanding. Your prayer request becomes more specific and calculated. You wouldn't be praying amiss. This way it is easier to tell when God is answering your prayer. Also, if you are a man/woman of understanding, you are most likely going to have played your part in getting what you want, therefore you would be praying about things that are beyond your capacity to deliver. This is the area for God to deliver. It's exactly what is meant by doing your best and leaving the rest.

To experience grace and be able to please God with ease, you need to be a righteous man and a man of faith. We have established that there is no righteousness or faith without understanding and we have now established that understanding is the key element to overcoming challenges in life.

This is how grace would make the life of an individual; any man/woman who is experiencing grace (pleasing God with ease or found pleasing to God) must first be a man of faith. Since faith is built on understanding, then such an individual would be a man/woman full of understanding. Thus, such a person would be able to overcome more of life's challenges than most people.

GRACE THROUGH THE GOSPEL

According to John, we get grace through the teachings of Jesus Christ.

John 1:17 - KJV

17.   For the law was given by Moses, but grace and truth came by Jesus Christ.

This means that because of what Jesus was teaching, we now have the power to overcome sin and live righteously with ease (we now have the power to please God with ease).

The question now becomes, what was Jesus teaching that gives us the power to please God with ease?

There are many debates on the ministry of Jesus, many people don't seem to agree on what Jesus's mission on earth was. But if you read the gospels in the bible, there is only one time Jesus expressly states what his assignment is.

Luke 4:43 - KJV

43. And he said unto them, I must preach the kingdom of God to other cities also: for therefore am I sent.

Thus, Jesus specifically states that this is his assignment: to preach the gospel of the kingdom of God. But before we proceed in this chapter, I would like to let you take note that there is no difference between the kingdom of God and the kingdom of heaven. The only thing is that in the book of Mathew, the kingdom of heaven is used while the other three gospels make use of the kingdom of God to mean the same thing. This is evident in the fact that the same story that is told in Mathew would say the kingdom of heaven while the other gospels would say the kingdom of God while narrating the same story.

Matthew 4:17 - KJV

*17.   From that time Jesus began to preach, and to say, Repent: for the **kingdom of heaven** is at hand.*

Mark 1:14-15 - KJV

*14.   Now after that John was put in prison, Jesus came into Galilee, preaching the gospel of the **kingdom of God**,*
*15.   And saying, The time is fulfilled, and the **kingdom of God** is at hand: repent ye, and believe the gospel.*

The verses above, do not only show that the kingdom of God and the kingdom of heaven are used interchangeably, but they also show the gospel preached by Jesus. However, the dispute or the confusion about the gospel of Jesus comes mostly from Luke 17:21.

Luke 17:20-21 - KJV

20.   And when he was demanded of the Pharisees, when the kingdom of God should come, he answered them and said, The kingdom of God cometh not with observation:
*21.   Neither shall they say, Lo here! or, lo there! for, behold, the **kingdom of God is within you**.*

The problem or confusion here is that Jesus said that the kingdom of God was inside a person. This has led to a big argument about the kingdom of God. Many Christians believe that the kingdom of God is a place where true Christians go after they die. But some other Christians and theologians argue that it is not a place. I am on the side of the latter. I believe that those who think that Jesus was talking about a place are wrong and are flirting with ignorance.

If you look at the gospel preached by Jesus in Matthew 4:17 and Mark 1:14-15, you would observe that Jesus also says that the kingdom of God is at hand. If you say something is at hand, you mean that the thing is in one's possession. To put it literally, you are saying that the person has it in his/her hands. This correlates with the statement that the kingdom of God is within You. If the kingdom of God was a place, how can it be within a person and how can it be in someone's hands or possession?

The answer is simple, the kingdom of God that Jesus was talking about isn't a place. If the kingdom of God isn't a place, then what is it?

After asking God this same question for a long time, I got my answer one morning in the most unlikely of manners. God simply reminded me of my biology class in secondary school. When living organisms were divided based on their character and nature, they were divided into kingdoms. According to biologists, the five kingdom categories of living organisms are Protista (the single-celled eukaryotes); Fungi (fungus and related organisms); Plantae (the plants); Animalia (the animals); Monera (the prokaryotes). This means the word kingdom could have been used to describe characteristics or ways of life or nature at some time in history.

I decided to put this interpretation into the bible and then I finally got the understanding I was looking for. If the word kingdom means characteristics/way of life/nature, then let us use this new understanding to interpret the teachings of Jesus and see if they explain things better.

Matthew 6:33 - KJV

*33.   But seek ye first the **kingdom of God,** and his righteousness; and all these things shall be added unto you.*

This verse could mean, seek ye first the character/nature/way of life of God; and all these things shall be added unto you.

Luke 4:43 - KJV

43.   And he said unto them, I must preach the kingdom of God to other cities also: for therefore am I sent.

This verse therefore means, I must preach the character/way of life/behaviour of God to other cities also: for therefore am I sent.

Matthew 4:17 - KJV

17. From that time Jesus began to preach, and to say, Repent: for the kingdom of heaven is at hand.

Mark 1:14-15 - KJV

14. Now after that John was put in prison, Jesus came into Galilee, preaching the gospel of the kingdom of God,
15. And saying, The time is fulfilled, and the **kingdom of God is at hand:** *repent ye, and believe the gospel.*

These verses will therefore mean that Jesus was saying repent for the nature/character/way of life/behaviour of God is in your possession. This begins to make a lot of sense when you consider Luke 10:20-21.

Luke 17:20-21 - KJV

20. And when he was demanded of the Pharisees, when the kingdom of God should come, he answered

them and said, The kingdom of God cometh not with observation:
*21.   Neither shall they say, Lo here! or, lo there! for, behold, **the kingdom of God is within you.***

These verses, therefore, mean that Jesus was saying that the nature/character/way of life/behaviour of God is within you. This also gets interesting when you observe that Jesus wasn't even talking to his disciples in this verse, he was talking to Pharisees. How could he have told the Pharisees that the kingdom of God was within them?

Another writer in the bible that seems to share this understanding about the kingdom of God is the author of the book of Romans.

Romans 14:17 - KJV

17. For the kingdom of God is not meat and drink; but righteousness, and peace, and joy in the Holy Ghost.

This verse will therefore mean that the nature of God is not in meat and drink; but righteousness peace and joy.

Unfortunately, many people think that Jesus was talking about a place when he was talking about the kingdom of God/Heaven. In reality, he was talking about the nature/way of life of God. Considering that he said the kingdom of God is at hand and within a person, Jesus was just preaching the same thing as Moses: every man has the nature of God deep inside of him.

There is therefore no difference between the gospel of Jesus and the teaching of Moses that man was created in the image of God.

Jesus was just an example of what man would be if he realized who he is (man has the nature/kingdom of God inside him) and lived the way he was created to be.

Jesus simply knew who he was, that is why he referred to himself as God and lived accordingly.

Jesus was also trying to tell people who they were. This is why when they accused him of claiming to be God, he also told them that they were Gods also.

John 10:34 - KJV

34. Jesus answered them, Is it not written in your law, I said, Ye are gods?

Most of the teachings of Jesus are built on this understanding. Most of the parables about the kingdom of God that Jesus gave was just Jesus trying to highlight one unique virtue about the kingdom of God (the nature of God/the way of life of God).

Matthew 5:3 - KJV

3. Blessed are the poor in spirit: for theirs is the kingdom of heaven.

In this verse, Jesus is simply saying blessed are the humble for theirs is the nature/life of God. Indirectly saying that the nature/life of God is a nature/life of humility. And those who are humble are expressing this nature.

Matthew 5:10 - KJV

10. Blessed are they which are persecuted for righteousness' sake: for theirs is the kingdom of heaven.

In this verse, Jesus was simply saying that the kingdom/life of God/character of God endures persecution for righteousness' sake.

In the case of the ten virgins, Jesus was just likening the kingdom of God (the way of life of God) to a way of life of wisdom that plans for the future.

Matthew 25:1-13 - KJV

1.   Then shall the kingdom of heaven be likened unto ten virgins, which took their lamps, and went forth to meet the bridegroom.
2.   And five of them were wise, and five were foolish.
3.   They that were foolish took their lamps, and took no oil with them:
4.   But the wise took oil in their vessels with their lamps.
5.   While the bridegroom tarried, they all slumbered and slept.
6.   And at midnight there was a cry made, Behold, the bridegroom cometh; go ye out to meet him.
7.   Then all those virgins arose, and trimmed their lamps. 8. And the foolish said unto the wise, Give us of your oil; for our lamps are gone out.

9.   But the wise answered, saying, Not so; lest there be not enough for us and you: but go ye rather to them that sell, and buy for yourselves.
10.   And while they went to buy, the bridegroom came; and they that were ready went in with him to the marriage: and the door was shut.
11.   Afterward came also the other virgins, saying, Lord, Lord, open to us.
12.   But he answered and said, Verily I say unto you, I know you not.
13.   Watch therefore, for ye know neither the day nor the hour wherein the Son of man cometh.

In the parable of the kingdom of God and talents, Jesus was teaching that the nature of God/ way of life of God/character of God makes use of the gifts given to them by God. The way of God does not condone laziness.

Matthew 25:14-30 - KJV

14.   For the kingdom of heaven is as a man travelling into a far country, who called his own servants, and delivered unto them his goods.

15.   And unto one he gave five talents, to another two, and to another one; to every man according to his several ability; and straightway took his journey.

16.   Then he that had received the five talents went and traded with the same, and made them other five talents.

17.   And likewise he that had received two, he also gained other two.

18.   But he that had received one went and digged in the earth, and hid his lord's money.

19.   After a long time the lord of those servants cometh, and reckoneth with them.

20.   And so he that had received five talents came and brought other five talents, saying, Lord, thou deliveredst unto me five talents: behold, I have gained beside them five talents more.

21.   His lord said unto him, Well done, thou good and faithful servant: thou hast been faithful over a few things, I will make thee ruler over many things: enter thou into the joy of thy lord.

22.   He also that had received two talents came and said, Lord, thou deliveredst unto me two talents: behold, I have gained two other talents beside them.

23.   His lord said unto him, Well done, good and faithful servant; thou hast been faithful over a few things, I will make thee ruler over many things: enter thou into the joy of thy lord.

24.   Then he which had received the one talent came and said, Lord, I knew thee that thou art an hard man, reaping where thou hast not sown, and gathering where thou hast not strawed:

25.   And I was afraid, and went and hid thy talent in the earth: lo, there thou hast that is thine.

26.   His lord answered and said unto him, Thou wicked and slothful servant, thou knewest that I reap where I sowed not, and gather where I have not strawed:

27.   Thou oughtest therefore to have put my money to the exchangers, and then at my coming I should have received mine own with usury.

28.   Take therefore the talent from him, and give it unto him which hath ten talents.

29.   For unto every one that hath shall be given, and he shall have abundance: but from him that hath not shall be taken away even that which he hath.

30.   And cast ye the unprofitable servant into outer darkness: there shall be weeping and gnashing of teeth.

This is also in line with God's instruction to man to be fruitful in Genesis 1:28.

Genesis 1:28 – KJV

28.   And God blessed them, and God said unto them, Be fruitful, and multiply, and replenish the earth, and subdue it: and have dominion over the fish of the sea, and over the fowl of the air, and over every living thing that moveth upon the earth.

If you observe closely, you would notice that before God gave man his assignments, he blessed them. In other words, he gave them gifts just like in Matthew 25:14-15. Thus, Jesus and Moses were hinting at the same thing.

In the parable of the labourer, where different labourers resumed work at different times, but the man who hired them had to pay the same wages, Jesus was just teaching that in the way of life/ kingdom/culture/character of God, one keeps to his agreements with others.

Matthew 20:1-16 - KJV

1.   For the kingdom of heaven is like unto a man that is an householder, which went out early in the morning to hire labourers into his vineyard.
2.   And when he had agreed with the labourers for a penny a day, he sent them into his vineyard.
3.   And he went out about the third hour, and saw others standing idle in the marketplace,
4.   And said unto them; Go ye also into the vineyard, and whatsoever is right I will give you.

And they went their way.

5.   Again he went out about the sixth and ninth hour, and did likewise.
6.   And about the eleventh hour he went out, and found others standing idle, and saith unto them, Why stand ye here all the day idle?
7.   They say unto him, Because no man hath hired us. He saith unto them, Go ye also into the vineyard; and whatsoever is right, that shall ye receive.
8.   So when even was come, the lord of the vineyard saith unto his steward, Call the labourers, and give them their hire, beginning from the last unto the first.
9.   And when they came that were hired about the eleventh hour, they received every man a penny.
10.   But when the first came, they supposed that they should have received more; and they likewise received every man a penny.

11.   And when they had received it, they murmured against the goodman of the house,

12.   Saying, These last have wrought but one hour, and thou hast made them equal unto us, which have borne the burden and heat of the day.

13.   But he answered one of them, and said, Friend, I do thee no wrong: didst not thou agree with me for a penny?

14.   Take that thine is, and go thy way: I will give unto this last, even as unto thee.

15.   Is it not lawful for me to do what I will with mine own? Is thine eye evil, because I am good?

16.   So the last shall be first, and the first last: for many be called, but few chosen.

If you carefully analyze all the teachings about the Kingdom of God/Heaven given by Jesus, you would see that he was just highlighting one good quality of God. In one parable he would highlight humility, in another, he would highlight justice and in another, forgiveness (for instance in the case of the prodigal son). In all his messages, he always likens the kingdom of God to these virtues.

Unfortunately, we will not be the first generation to think that Jesus was talking of a physical place when he was speaking about the kingdom of God. The Pharisees thought it was a place that is why one of them had to ask him where it will be and when it will come. But Jesus told them that the "kingdom of God is within you".

In today's evangelical Christianity, people are still making the same mistake that the Pharisees made talking about the kingdom of God as a place where there will be physical partying and feasting. I do not blame those who have made this mistake though, they only failed to recognize the use of idioms or figures of speech in the New Testament. For example, we are seeing that the kingdom of God doesn't mean a physical kingdom but it means a lifestyle/nature/character. Another idiom that is often misunderstood is the phrase "mansions in my father's house" which also shares meaning with the kingdom of God in a way. In both cases, Jesus was talking about a lifestyle/way of life/nature/mindset/characteristics/experience that isn't of this world but liveable in this world. Jesus was just pointing at a life of righteousness, peace, and joy. Jesus was using the word mansion to speak of the benefits of the kingdom/life of God. These benefits are righteousness peace and Joy.

The writer of the book of Romans seems to have understood Jesus and was also trying to correct the misconception that many people have concerning the kingdom of God. This writer was trying to correct the idea that the kingdom of God is a place where there is endless partying and feasting.

Romans 14:17 - KJV

17. For the kingdom of God is not meat and drink; but righteousness, and peace, and joy in the Holy Ghost.

If you observe closely, this writer says that the kingdom of God is not in meat and drink, indirectly saying it is not that partying and feasting that people think it is, but it is righteousness, peace, and joy. This means the nature/life of God is one of righteousness peace and Joy.

When Jesus was teaching his disciples how to pray, he taught them to say "thy kingdom come that thy will be done on earth as in the heavens". If the kingdom was a place, how would he be praying that that place should come to the earth so that the will of God be done on the earth? Jesus was simply teaching his disciples to pray for the kingdom/nature/life/character/mindset of God so that they can be able to fulfil the will of God on the earth. If you take a closer look at the teaching of the lord's prayer you would realize that he wasn't talking about a place when he spoke about the kingdom of God.

Luke 11:2 - KJV

2.   And he said unto them, When ye pray, say, Our Father which art in heaven, Hallowed be thy name. Thy kingdom come. Thy will be done, as in heaven, so in earth.

Anytime you see the kingdom of God being referenced or feasting and enjoyment being referenced in terms of the kingdom of God, just understand that they are expressions of a life of righteousness, peace, and joy. John in the book of revelations makes use of these expressions a lot. This is why the book of revelations has been difficult to understand for many.

1 Corinthians 15:50 - KJV

50. Now this I say, brethren, that flesh and blood cannot inherit the kingdom of God; neither doth corruption inherit incorruption.

By saying that the flesh and blood cannot inherit the kingdom of God, this writer seems to understand that the Kingdom of God is not a place where we go physically. This also throws shade on the doctrines that teach that the kingdom of God is a place you go after you die because first of all, you dump your body when you die. Also, by using the word inherit, this means the kingdom of God is something that we get due to some right that we have just like a child having the right to his father's properties. This means we have the right to the kingdom of God and it is our inheritance. But since we do not inherit it in our flesh and blood, we, therefore, inherit it in our spirit man. Also, if it is an inheritance, it means we already have the right to it. This is what Jesus was saying when he said that the kingdom of God is within you or is at hand.

Thus, the kingdom of God (nature of God) is one we inherited from God our father as a result of being his children (created in his image). This further drives home my earlier statement that it is the spirit that takes the nature and mind of God while the flesh takes that of the Waters and the Earth (this world).

Now that we have an idea of what the kingdom of God is, let us revisit the gospel preached by Jesus.

Mark 1:14-15 - KJV

14.   Now after that John was put in prison, Jesus came into Galilee, preaching the gospel of the kingdom of God,
15.   And saying, The time is fulfilled, and the kingdom of God is at hand: repent ye, and believe the gospel.

The other keyword in the gospel is the word repent.

We generally have a good idea of what repent means, especially from a religious point of view.

To repent means to feel or express sincere regret about one's wrongdoing or sin.

However, there is a broader, ancient and non-religious use of the word repent which is still similar in a way to the religious use of the word.

Repent can also be used to mean a change of heart/mind towards an idea or something or a decision. This means a person can repent from a choice or a belief system. Repentance is just to change one's mind about something. Let me show you a broader use of the word repent in the early books of the bible.

Exodus 13:17 - KJV

17.   And it came to pass, when Pharaoh had let the people go, that God led them not through the way of the land of the Philistines, although that was near; for God said, Lest peradventure the people repent when they see war, and they return to Egypt:

This is the first use of the word repent in the bible. Notice how it is used slightly different from modern-day use. In this story, God led the children of Israel through a longer route when they left Egypt because the shorter route might lead them into the paths of other nations who might decide to fight them. God knew that they were mentally not ready for any war and that if they were faced with one, they would most likely change their mind (repent) and go back to Egypt. God did not want them to change their mind (repent) and go back to Egypt. Take note that the word repent in this verse is even used to indicate a negative decision that the children of Israel would have made if they were faced with war. This shows that they could repent into going back to bondage.

The word repent simply means to change one's mind/perception/ thinking, whether it's from sin or from another thing, it is dependent on the situation.

To bring this understanding back to the gospel of Jesus, we can safely say Jesus was simply saying that a change of mind is needed. Therefore, Jesus knew that the problem of man is a mental one, one that needs man to change the way he thinks.

But in the case of the gospel of Jesus, man needs to change the way he thinks concerning the kingdom of God.

In other words, Jesus was simply saying to the people that they have the kingdom of God/nature of God/character of God/life of God/ in their possession (at hand), therefore they should change the way they think about themselves. They should stop seeing the kingdom of God as something far from them.

Matthew 4:17 - KJV

17.   From that time Jesus began to preach, and to say, Repent: for the kingdom of heaven is at hand.

Mark 1:14-15 - KJV

14.   Now after that John was put in prison, Jesus came into Galilee, preaching the gospel of the kingdom of God,
15.   And saying, The time is fulfilled, and the kingdom of God is at hand: repent ye, and believe the gospel.

Jesus was saying that people need to start seeing themselves as people who have the nature of God inside of them (in their possession) if they were to start living right like God.

Jesus was simply saying the same thing that Moses was also saying. Man is created in the image of God but due to ignorance of who he is, man has been malfunctioning and thus lacking the life experience of righteousness, peace, and joy which are meant to be his right by virtue of being created in the image of God. It was this ignorance of self that made Eve believe the lies of the serpent.

So many people can't even imagine a world in which their natural reactions to things will be righteous and good. So many people cannot even entertain the idea that man can be good. This is all coming from the fact that they are ignorant of their capacity (that they possess the life of God inside of them).

We all at some point in our lives have been made to see ourselves wrongly as less than who we are (Gods) due to the kind of information circulating around us.

This ignorance of who we are is what has made us struggle to be righteous even to the point where many have given up on the possibility for man to be righteous. If only we understood that we are spirit beings who are created in his image and therefore have his kingdom(nature/capabilities) within us. If only we understood that we are not the flesh and that the flesh is just a physical container fashioned from this physical realm to house us (the spirit). We would not have inherited the identity, shortcomings, and desires of our flesh.

Unfortunately, we now look at ourselves as the flesh so we claim its shortcomings this is why we spend most of our lives trying to compensate by chasing earthly things that we think can make us better. In our pursuit for these earthly things, pleasures and recognitions, we get desperate enough to lie, steal, kill, fornicate, envy, and commit many evils. All because we do not understand who we are.

If we had understood the gospel of Jesus, we would have realized that physical measurements don't apply to us. We are spirit beings with the nature of God so we can't be defined by physical shortcomings or wealth, and the desires of the flesh are not our desires but just the flesh living up to its reputation. We would have been able to distance ourselves from the many troubles of the flesh and its desires. We would have found it easier to not be pushed by our flesh into sin. We would have found it easier to please God (grace).

Like I have said it is one thing to know something and it is another thing to understand it. We mostly knew the gospel preached by Jesus but we mostly did not understand it. And like we said in previous chapters it is understanding that leads to grace.

In summary, what John 1:17 was saying is that Moses brought laws but Jesus brought understanding through his message, an understanding that is meant to help us please God with ease (grace).

Unfortunately, our lack of this understanding has limited the way we think about ourselves and we have been acting accordingly.

Proverbs 23:7 - KJV

7.   *For as he thinketh in his heart, so is he: Eat and drink, saith he to thee; but his heart is not with thee.*

We have simply been living out how we think about ourselves in our hearts. This is due to ignorance of who we are. And it is written that we perish because of our ignorance.

Hosea 4:6 - KJV

6.   **My people are destroyed for lack of knowledge:** *because thou hast rejected knowledge, I will also reject thee, that thou shalt be no priest to me: seeing thou hast forgotten the law of thy God, I will also forget thy children.*

And there is no ignorance worse than ignorance of one's self. However, understanding the gospel preached by Jesus would have gotten rid of this ignorance.

SUMMARY

The summary of this book is simple, Grace is the ability to please God with ease, or the ability to be found pleasing by God with ease. Grace is the power over sin and the ability to overcome the flesh and its desires with ease. Therefore, if one is not experiencing victory over sin, such a person can't claim to be experiencing grace. Grace is something that is expressed via our victory over sin. This is the way to please God and find grace in his sight.

If you choose to see God's grace as a favour from God, you must realize that this favour is merited because every man/woman that found grace in the sight of God in the bible were people who were described as righteous in one way or the other. Their righteousness was the merit for the grace. Therefore, there is nothing unmerited about God's grace. It is earned through righteousness. This is why I have argued that grace is the evidence/consequence of righteousness.

Grace is the proof of faith and righteousness. And faith and righteousness can't exist without understanding. So, grace can't exist without understanding. Therefore, if you want to increase your expression of grace, then you need to increase your level of understanding.

What I am ultimately saying is that the ultimate thing an individual needs to be able to experience grace (please God) is understanding.

Proverb 4:7 - KJV

7.   Wisdom is the principal thing; therefore get wisdom: and with all thy getting get understanding.

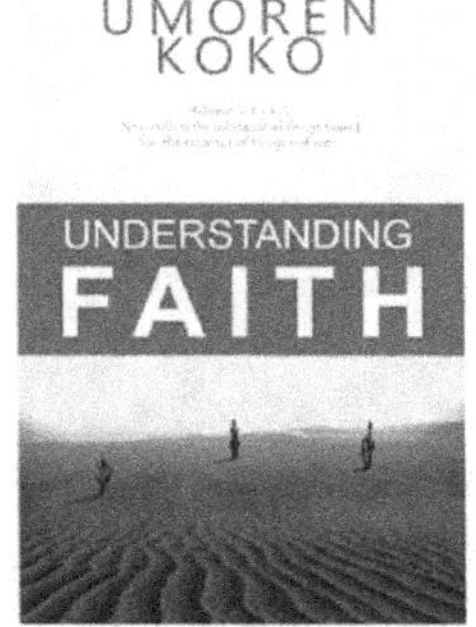

THE FREEDOM SERIES

This is a series of five
books designed to
free
your soul from the
control of the flesh
and the mindset of

sin.

Umoren Koko is a life coach, a teacher and an economist born in the city of Lagos in Nigeria. He has a first degree in Economics from Covenant University in Nigeria. He also has a Masters Degree in International Business And Management from Nottingham Trent University.
Motivated by the quest to understand life with the aim of helping people live a much simpler and fulfilling life, Koko has spent most of his adult years seeking to understand God and his ways so that he can be a medium for educating people on the things of God and Life.